Rachael — here's to adventure! Shelley 2010

ALASKA

SHELLEY GILL

PHOTOGRAPHS BY

PATRICK J. ENDRES

Charlesbridge

Big, wild, and bold;
rock, snow, and cold.
Wolves sing, bears prowl;
mountains soar, glaciers growl.

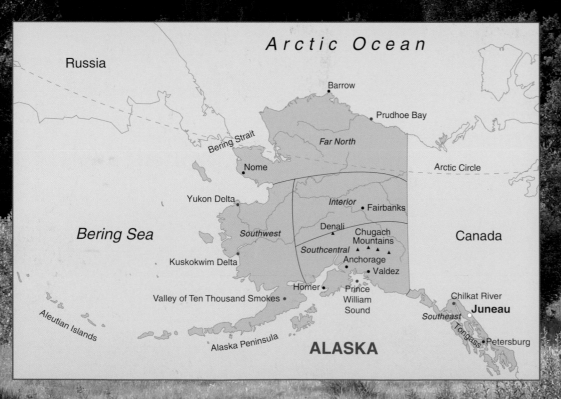

Arctic Ocean

Russia

Barrow

Prudhoe Bay

Bering Strait

Far North

Arctic Circle

Nome

Yukon Delta

Interior • Fairbanks

Bering Sea

Denali

Chugach
Mountains

Canada

Southwest

Southcentral

Anchorage
• Valdez

Kuskokwim Delta

Homer

Prince
William
Sound

Chilkat River

Valley of Ten Thousand Smokes

Juneau

Aleutian Islands

Southeast

Tongass

Alaska Peninsula

Petersburg

ALASKA

ALASKA.

Ice and snow, polar bears and outdoor potties, and all the people live in igloos? No way. Hulking gray blue mountains, dense rain forests, deserts of delicate alpine flowers, and oceans pierced by rivers of ice. The Aleut word for this place is *Alyeska*. It means "the Great Land."

And the 49th state *is* great. Sprawling near the top of the world, it is a place of extremes: extreme weather, extreme landscapes, extreme beauty.

Alaska is 586,412 square miles —one-fifth the size of the Lower 48 states. It has many different climates and more coastline than the rest of the United States. It also has the coldest average winter temperature of any state in the United States.

A newcomer to Alaska is called a cheechako.

Beams of light
rake the sky;
gold and green shiver
as winter sighs.

How would you like to live at the top of the world? In Barrow, Alaska, the sun sets in November and doesn't come up again until the middle of January. This polar night also occurs in other parts of northern Alaska and lasts for varying lengths of time.

No sunlight means it's cold, too! Winter temperatures in these Arctic regions can get down to sixty degrees below zero, and when the wind blows, the wind chill can be a hundred degrees below! Caribou and polar bears stay warm thanks to hollow hairs that provide them with extra insulation. People have a tougher time staying warm, as their nose hairs freeze and their spit shatters. Children bundle up in clothes of fur and fleece before heading out to recess in the moonlight.

But the cold's not the only cool thing up here. The dancing light show in the sky is called the aurora borealis. Also called the northern lights, the aurora is created when gas molecules in the upper atmosphere collide with solar electrons and protons trapped in the earth's magnetic field. This occurs about sixty-eight miles above the surface of the earth.

Icy lace on window sills,
glaciers grind fjords and hills.
Winter's weight stills the land.
Moonlight shimmers gold and grand.

Cheechako tip: Don't eat yellow snow.

Deep fjords point to receding glaciers, their icy blue tongues still busy at work carving valleys and molding mountains. Ice covers nearly thirty thousand square miles of Alaska. Receding glaciers leave pockets of ice that melt, dotting the land north of the Chugach Mountains with thousands of lakes and ponds. In winter, snow covers most of Alaska. The deepest snow in Alaska is at Thompson Pass near Valdez. It snows about thirty-six feet every winter. That's as tall as a four-story building!

"Seward's Folly"
they called the deal,
but for $7.2 million,
the cost was a steal!

Cheechako tip: Ask for a gold nugget in the store and you get a potato. Ask for a moose nugget and you get moose poop.

In the early 1700s, a Danish explorer, Vitus Bering, led a series of imperial expeditions for Russia. Because of these expeditions, the Russians claimed Alaska as their own territory. During the next hundred years, fur trappers were lured north, along with whalers who sailed up the Bering Strait in the 1840s.

United States Secretary of State William Seward convinced the government to buy Alaska from Russia. The deal was sealed on March 30, 1867. People who thought it was a waste of money called Alaska "Seward's Folly" or "Seward's Icebox," but the scoffing stopped when gold was discovered along Anvil Creek near Nome in 1898. The rush was on.

Fox crouches in cold, dark rocks;
caribou chip lichen blocks.
Polar bear stalks ringed seals;
winds whine, raven wheels.

Cheechako tip: Don't let go of the sled.

As the spring sun skims the Arctic horizon, the fox returns to her den. The caribou keep a wary eye on wolves trailing the herd, and on the pack ice, the polar bear patiently waits at the breathing hole of a ringed seal. In Alaska there are more animals than people.

By March the snow is deep, the days are long, and it's time to play. Alaskans skate, ski, snowshoe, snowmobile, mountain bike, and of course, drive dogs.

The roots of this most famous northern sport lie in the lifestyle of the Native Alaskan people. Dog driving, or mushing, began thousands of years ago, when a barely-domesticated wolf was first hooked to a sled. Now teams of sled-pulling huskies race across thousands of miles of winter trails. Mushers' faces sprout "snotsicles" while their dogs prance along in fleece booties. The 1,150-mile Iditarod and the 1,000-mile Yukon Quest are two races that make dog mushing Alaska's state sport.

Valleys and mountains
bloom in spring.
Geese, swans, and cranes,
stirring with wings.

It's spring in Alaska's Interior. The warmer weather causes the snow to melt in the spindly white and black spruce forests. These forests are called "taiga," meaning "land of little sticks."

Rivers that created highways of ice for winter travelers now provide nesting grounds for the migratory birds of spring. The Yukon and Kuskokwim deltas are home to cranes, swans, ducks, and geese, as well as five species of salmon that make up the heart of the food chain for a variety of mammals, including grizzly and black bears.

Black bears aren't always black, and brown bears aren't always brown. Black bears can have brown, cinnamon, spotted, or even blue fur! Blue-fur black bears are called glacier bears. Brown bears have dark brown to light blond fur — oh, and a big old hump on their back.

The *Exxon Valdez* runs aground;
the sea burns black and thick;
oozing oil poisons the Sound.
We have made Alaska sick.

Good Friday, March 24, 1989, was a good day for tears. That was the day the oil tanker *Exxon Valdez* ran aground on Bligh Reef in Prince William Sound. Because many safety procedures had been ignored, little could be done to stop the environmental disaster that followed. Alaskans flocked to beaches, trying to save dying wildlife, including hundreds of thousands of birds coated in oil. Almost two decades after the spill, and despite millions spent in clean-up costs, the oil still seeps from the shore gravel in Prince William Sound.

Cheechako tip: Spring is called "breakup."

One quarter of the oil the United States produces comes from Alaska. The giant tankers fill up at Valdez, the end of a pipeline that begins eight hundred miles north at the Prudhoe Bay oil fields.

Ring of Fire explodes;
erupting lava steams.
Earthquakes rattle
this land of extremes.

Cheechako tip: Don't ski on slopes where there are no trees.

Colliding land masses and grinding glaciers created the Alaska we see today. More than forty volcanoes let off plenty of steam, most of them in the Aleutian Range, where the Pacific plate dives under the North American plate.

The largest volcanic eruption of the 20th century occurred June 5–8, 1912, creating what is now called the Valley of Ten Thousand Smokes in Katmai National Park on the Alaska Peninsula. Native people fled their villages in boats, fearing the end of the world.

On March 27, 1964, Alaska was shattered by an earthquake with a magnitude of 9.2 on the Richter scale—the strongest ever felt in North America. The epicenter was forty miles from Valdez. The quake killed fifteen people, and tidal waves smashed whole towns to pieces, killing another 110 people.

Summer explodes
with light and heat!
Bears and whales
gotta eat! Gotta eat!

Cheechako tip: Don't clean your fish near your tent, and don't wipe your hands on the pants you intend to use as a pillow.

Summer comes to Alaska in an explosion of life. In Barrow the sun never sets between May and July. The Great Land becomes the Land of the Midnight Sun.

All over Alaska the pulse of the land quickens as the last river ice crashes its way to the sea. This is the season of birth: delicate flowers push through leftover ice and bloom, streams are alive with salmon fry, and geese and cranes honk overhead, while people frantically mend fishing nets and set out to sea. Arctic animals' coats of winter-white fur turn to brown or gray. Walruses haul out on islands in the Bering Sea, while brown bear sows dig clams with twin cubs in tow. Caribou push north onto their summer range, their wide, fur-fringed hooves supporting them in the mud as well as they did in the snow. Moose calves teeter on stilt legs, blinking their enormous eyes.

Summer is short and so sweet. Farmers grow hundred-pound cabbages and torpedo-sized zucchini in the long daylight, and everyone else loads up the camping gear and mosquito repellent and heads for the Bush.

Early summer also sees the chocolate lily in bloom— but it's no treat. The lilies are called "stinky diapers" because, well, that's what they smell like. These stinkers are pollinated by beetles and flies that prefer noxious odors.

High, high, high . . .
Denali—top of the world.
Fly, fly, fly . . .
eagles loop and whirl.

Alaska is full of natural extremes. Denali National Park is named after the highest mountain in North America. The Tanana Indians named the mountain Denali, which means "the Great One." The U.S. Congress changed the name to Mt. McKinley after our 25th president, but Alaskans simply call it "The Mountain." At 20,320 feet, it is so huge it creates its own weather and dominates the skyline from Anchorage to the Interior.

In summer the top layer of soil thaws, and plant life thrives. Denali provides animals and their young with a place to feed and fatten up for the harsh winter ahead.

Cheechako tip: Be careful where you step. Some mudflats are quicksand.

Voices chant a hunting tale;
Raven creates moon and tides.
Strong teeth soften
stiff walrus hides.

About twelve thousand years ago, North America's first settlers crossed a land bridge that stretched between Asia and Alaska. These people traveled frigid grassland steppes, hunting the woolly mammoth, caribou, and steppe bison.

Alaska is home to many Native people, including the Athabascan Indians in the Interior, the Yup'ik in the west, the Iñupiaq in the north and northwest, the Aleuts and Alutiq on the Alaska Peninsula and islands beyond, and the Eyak, Tlingit, Haida, and Tsimshian on the southeast coast.

Alaska Natives have distinct languages and cultures. Animal skin sewing, basket weaving, ivory carving, and beadwork are just some of the skills practiced today. The Tlingit perform spiritual dances in honor of their elders. The Haida, Tsimshian, and Tlingit are all well known for their totem pole carvings. The Iñupiaq perform the "blanket toss" at their June whaling celebration. These traditions are passed from generation to generation as a way of preserving the Native way of life.

Bush planes zip up the coast;
nets bulge with sockeye salmon;
gold dust hides in frigid creeks,
ready for the panning.

There are few roads in Alaska—and, in the Southeast, none that connect Juneau, Alaska's capital, with the rest of the state. Here travel is by air. When the weather goes bad, the isolation is complete.

Most of the Southeast lies in the nation's largest national forest, the Tongass. A temperate rain forest, the Tongass is home to the world's largest population of brown bears. It is also rich in marine life, such as otters, seals, and sea lions. During the summer several species of whales migrate to feed in the waters of the Tongass.

The biggest halibut on record was caught in Petersburg, located on Mitkof Island. It weighed 495 pounds.

Catching a big halibut, known as a "barn door," is like trying to drag up the ocean bottom.

Cheechako tip: Airmail means just that—the pilot drops your mail out of the plane . . .

. . . and it flies through the air and lands in the lake.

N4794C

Alaska Seaplanes

Tail prints widen
on a sea of glass.
Whoosh! goes a blow
as the whales swim past.

A lot of people think Alaska is all ice and snow, but that's not true. In the Interior a hot sunny day can be one hundred degrees! In the Southeast, summers are cool, with temperatures in the fifties and rain, rain, rain. Taku winds sweep off glaciers and howl across the Inside Passage, stirring waves that keep boats at anchor.

Many species of whales migrate to Alaska for the rich food. Baleen whales feast on krill and herring, while orcas eat larger animals. The narwhal lives in the Arctic. Males, and some females, have a spiral tusk about seven feet long, which grows through their upper lip.

There are more than four hundred species of birds in Alaska. One hundred million seabirds travel here each summer to either breed or find food. The Chilkat River is known for its huge bald eagle population. Thousands of eagles gather to feed on a late run of chum salmon.

Cheechako tip: Stay upwind from whales; they exhale what Alaskans call "fish farts."

Fall.
Fireweed and fish camp.
Beautiful, brief autumn;
brown fur goes white,
birds head south,
hunting and hibernation.

Cheechako tip:
Alaskan definition of luggage:
two cardboard boxes sealed with duct tape.

Fireweed blazes and blueberry bushes leave the hillsides bleeding crimson. Red is the color of death, signaling winter is only weeks away. But fall may be the busiest season in the North. Geese and cranes spiral upward by the thousands to head south. Moose and deer begin the rut season. It's almost time for male caribou to shed their antlers. Animals are moving, and not far behind are the hunters. Bears and wolves and man need the short weeks to prepare for the long dark ahead.

Fish are hung to smoke, berries find their way to the freezer, and rifles are cleaned. Wood and more wood is chopped and stacked. The sea turns gray and the tides and winds push fierce waves against shores of pan ice. And in the early morning, frost tickles the last birch leaves from their limbs.

Beyond the skyline of Alaska's urban lands,
with fast food and street lamps and spilled trash cans,
the stark blue curves of the Chugach mountains loom,
as the bald eagle spirals to his autumn tune.

While some Alaskans live in the bush, trapping for furs, fishing, or panning for gold, most kids live in cities. Kids in Anchorage are just like kids anywhere else: they get ready for school to start each fall, hang out at the mall, and eat at McDonald's. Anchorage could be Anywhere, USA—until you see the Chugach Mountains rising over the city, or pass a thousand-pound moose strolling down Northern Lights Boulevard. Fall in Alaska is short. The colors quickly fade, and snow is just around the corner.

When you talk about Alaska, everything is bigger and more. The tallest mountain, the biggest earthquake, the biggest bears, the longest days, the darkest nights, the most wilderness. Alaska is indeed "the Great Land," America's Last Frontier.

Cheechako tip: When Alaskans leave the state, they say they are "going Outside."

Text copyright © 2007 by Shelley Gill
Photographs copyright © 2007 by Patrick J. Endres/AlaskaPhotoGraphics.com
Map copyright © 1995 by Cartesia Software. All rights reserved.
All rights reserved, including the right of reproduction in whole
or in part in any form. Charlesbridge and colophon are registered
trademarks of Charlesbridge Publishing, Inc.

Published by Charlesbridge
85 Main Street
Watertown, MA 02472
(617) 926-0329
www.charlesbridge.com

Library of Congress Cataloging-in-Publication Data
Gill, Shelley.
    Alaska / Shelley Gill ; photographs by Patrick J. Endres.
       p. cm.
    ISBN 978-0-88106-292-2 (reinforced for library use)
    ISBN 978-0-88106-293-9 (softcover)
1. Alaska—Juvenile literature. I. Endres, Patrick J. II. Title.
F904.3.G48 2007
979.8—dc22   2006009020

Printed in China
(hc) 10 9 8 7 6 5 4 3 2 1
(sc) 10 9 8 7 6 5 4 3 2 1

Photographs were taken with Canon professional film
  and high resolution digital SLR cameras.
Display type and text type set in Ogre and Cheltenham
Color separations by Chroma Graphics, Singapore
Printed and bound by Jade Productions
Production supervision by Brian G. Walker
Designed by Diane M. Earley

For Sandy Cronland, Libby Riddles, Becky Howard, Olga Von Z, Joyanna, Sam, Julia, Janet, Tiara and Trek—all wild, wonderful women of the north. And a special thanks to Jane Fox of St. Andrews, Scotland, for not putting me in time-out.

—S. G.

For Ryan and Cooper, and all the little people in my life who teach me through their bright eyes and sense of wonder.

—P. J. E.

Cheechako tip: Wave a flashlight at the mail train and it will stop for you.